Advance Uncorrected Proof

Author __Andrew Harvey__

Title __NO DIAMONDS, NO HAT,__

__NO HONEY__

Probable Publication Date: __April 29, 1985__

Probable Price: __$13.95 Cl,__

☐ Illustrations
☐ Index
☐ Bibliography
☐ Appendix
☐ Glossary
☐ Other front or back matter

Dual Ed

Sent by __M. Rusoff__

☑ Publicity Department   ☐ Sales Department

Houghton Mifflin Co.

ANDREW HARVEY
NO DIAMONDS, NO HAT, NO HONEY

by the same author

poetry
WINTER SCARECROW
MASKS AND FACES
EVIDENCE .
HOMAGE TO TOUKARAM
THE FABIUS POEMS
A FULL CIRCLE

translations
(with Anne Pennington)
MACEDONIAN SONGS
BLAZHE KONESKY (SELECTED POEMS)
THE GOLDEN APPLE

non-fiction
A JOURNEY IN LADAKH

Andrew Harvey

NO DIAMONDS, NO HAT, NO HONEY

Boston
Houghton Mifflin Company

ISBN 395-36977   Code 6-87402 C1
ISBN 395-36978   Code 6-87403 Pa

First published 1984
Copyright © Andrew Harvey 1984

Printed in the United States of America

The drawings on pages 3, 8 and 72 are
by Emma Chichester Clark.

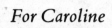

For Caroline

'What we know must be known to its roots, for we shall never know anything until we know its causes. There can be no knowledge until knowing reaches the hidden reasons. Thus, too, life cannot be perfect until it has returned to its secret source, where life is Being, a life the soul receives when it dies down to its roots so that we might live that life beyond which itself is Being.'

Meister Eckhart

'Leave thy damnable faces, and begin.'

Hamlet

I

' "Bitter as the winter wind traditionally is, and bitter
As the first scent of magnolias is to those
In love but not loved, and bitter as the oboe can be
In any romantic orchestra, there is nothing as
    bitter . . . " '

'A grand beginning,' Lydia said, 'except
For that oboe-break – and the sorrowful syntax,'
The 'Palestrina effect', as she called it,
'It is sumptuous, all right; gives the right hurt.

You can write the old tunes when you want to!
Them old tunes! But how do they help?
You must dissolve that music,' she said. Her tone
Was not musical. 'You must take that oboe

And wring its neck. There must be no magnolias,
No syntax opening like a rose . . . '
She looks at me coldly . . .
' "Bitter as the winter wind traditionally is,

And bitter as the magnolias . . . " '
'The bitterness you really mean',
She breaks in, 'is terminal; nothing rises from it
That has not first been utterly burnt.'

9

II

'Soak a long time in the black suds
Of disaster and you'll come out –

This is Lydia's Law – ' she laughs, 'not clean exactly
But white, white of the ancient lies . . . '

She claps her hands. 'If you believe that,' she says,
'You'll believe anything.' And throws me down

From whatever Babel we are standing on, down
Into a lake of pitch

Where I can do nothing but drown
And where she reappears, very cheerful considering,

With a parasol, and in a boat with sails
As gaudy as Cleopatra's

Saying, 'Good, your forehead is darkening,'
And 'Thank god, I can no longer see

Those appalling trustful whites of your eyes.'

III

Lydia and the Eagle

'Don't just sit there gawping at it,' Lydia rasped,
'Go upstairs, take your position like a general,

Scan its wings, feather by feather,
Be imperial and study it

In the sharpest light. You are impossible,
So passive! Will I never train you?'

I obeyed (when do I not?) and went upstairs,
Chose my position (jutting out my chin)

Took out my waxy new glasses
Stood (with my legs apart) like Napoleon.

The eagle knew nothing of all this, naturally,
Flew away almost as soon as I

Started to look at him. No use saying, 'The eagle
Hung above the blue lake,' 'The lake was blessed

By the perfect circling of the eagle,' although
Both were honourable sentences, clean feelings,

The eagle was not there. I was angry,
'Why didn't you leave me in peace?

I could have watched the eagle silently
And in my own time.'

Lydia turned at the door: 'Why did you listen to me?'
Smiling, for my taste, far too broadly.

IV

'In fairy stories,' Lydia said,
'I am only interested
In what happens to the villains.

Look . . . the stepmother suddenly becoming
Radiant and forgiving,
Wearing white and scenting her breath with spring,
Is that plausible?

The witch being shoved into the oven
And cooked into a sweet –
Isn't that a little neat?

In the stories I love,'
Said Lydia,
'The wicked stay wicked
And laugh in the face of the Good
And live out to the end their doom.

Stories should make us tremble, like life does – '
Lighting a lamp and taking out her cards –

'Shall we see who will suffer tonight and who will die?'

V

Lydia as Hecuba

'All suffering to me now is camp, frankly.
When you're changed to a dog, you see
The world hilariously.

So many nightclubs gone. The town quite flat.
I am a dog that wears a hat
A clown's hat at that –

Naturally I am left alone.
No, I don't blame anyone.
And I have this bone

To gnaw on still. What a joke! Tasteless too . . .
But what am I to do
With no words left, and only one mouth?

I could wear knickers, I could go south,
I could write to the papers saying
Oh, god knows what, or start praying –

But who would I pray to and what would I say?
Now *that's* the only serious line.
I cannot say the word "Divine"

Without my lips and knockers turning black.
Is that naughty of me,
Is it wicked, or a lack?

God may be a star to others, but to me
He is Death, and then some, frankly.
Death, Death, Death and no one

Listening, and even the screams turning camp.
There, I've used "camp" again.
Ah, darlings, the pain! –

If "camp" could be a "lamp"
To guide me through this crazy cave
I'd have no need to rave

And there'd be some hope for rhyme
But there isn't and that's that.
So sing it out bravely –

"Beyond tragedy,"
Like the holy wised-up queen I am –
The world is pointless, *fade*, and flat.

Répétez, mesdames et messieurs,
Ze world ees . . .
Good. Good. You belt it out well.
Now put a little heart into it, darlings,

So it hurts like hell.'

VI

The Last Thistle

'It is the last thing alive,' Lydia whispered. 'Look
At it. And at the dead purple sky around it.'

'You are the last thing alive,' I said, over and over,
Wanting to touch it so tenderly it would break into
   flower.

'You think you have healing hands,
You think just a touch from your hands . . .

But the world is dead . . .
So what will you do now?'

I took the thistle, I pressed it between my lips
Until they bled. How they bled!

Down my chin, down my arms, onto this page . . .
'Always the noisy gesture,' Lydia said,

'So even the last thing alive
Is not allowed its quiet.'

VII

As soon as I came towards her (dignifiedly, I thought,
My caftan weighted with celestial symbols)

She laughed. 'You're the Sphinx,' I sulked,
'You're not supposed to laugh.' 'God,' she said,

'If you could see yourself . . .
Where did you get those sandals?'

And was off again. My sandals? What could be wrong
With my sandals with their little wings?

'Damn my sandals,' I said, 'I've come all this way',
Pouting, 'to learn my destiny.'

'Destiny' was Lydia's cue, and, it must be said,
She folded her stone wings about her, and looked
    sphinx-like.

A desert wind began . . . And I? –
I felt expansive, even a little mystical

A minor Amerigo Vespucci of the spirit.
'Leave Vespucci out of it, get to the question.'

'No Lydia,' I say patiently, 'it isn't me
Who asks the questions, it's you . . .

Don't you know anything?' She starts to laugh again
And I, despite my sandals, the wind,

My Vespucci-like stirrings, approach
A state of hysteria.

'Approach?
You've lived in one for years.'

Then she is silent, the desert darkens . . .
'I can't stay here all night,

No mortal can stay in the desert and live,'
And other half-truths (but I really was shaking).

Still she says nothing, and still the wind . . .
I stroke my sandals for luck,

I summon all the strengths of my long despair,
Stride up to her, shout into her stone ear –

'Ask me now! I'm ready! I'm here!'
(Have I ever sounded braver, more mature?)

A noise begins from beneath her wings,
A noise like a thousand street-kids laughing . . .

And out of it soars Lydia's voice
Unnaturally sweet and clear –

'There is no question or secret, Fernando dear.'

VIII

Epiphany

'Don't let them in!' I screamed, but naturally Lydia
Did. And the Three Kings kneeled, one by one,

To an invisible consort of viols and sackbuts . . .
'God, the music!' I drawled, affecting detachment

As the viols twiddled out of key and the sackbuts
Wheezed and whistled menacingly.

Lydia was enchanted, spinning round and round in her
Print dress. I cried, 'No myrrh! Above all no myrrh!'

But myrrh poured from the black King's hands in clouds
And I was soon helpless, drunk on its fragrance,
   staggering,

While the other King hit me with his fist of gold twice,
Three times, what does it matter, and the third

(What thin legs he had!) ran round and round the room . . .
'Frankincense,' he shouted, 'frankincense!' as if it were

The only word he knew (which it may have been),
   desperate
He would be left out. Which he couldn't be.

For it was my day to be loaded with destiny.
They grabbed brandy and biscuits, and left.

I heard them whistling in the garden
Vulgarly, I thought, like a group of music-hall

Sailors. Lydia said, 'How do you feel?'
Knowing I was suicidal.

'I am the dove,' I moaned
'Found out in my secret place

With all my feathers plucked.' Lydia yawned.
'You asked', she said, 'for destiny.

You've got the juiciest I could find.' 'My love,
You are too cleverly kind . . . '

She was already on the table singing,
'Your evil shall become gold

Your self frankincense
Your spirit myrrh, o bitter perfume, that speaks

Of Death and Transcendence . . . '
She giggled. 'Death and Transcendence,

How *German*!! See how all the hoo-ha
Makes me chatter . . . '

Clutching her sides (they never looked so thin)
And saying in my voice,

'Take this cup from me! Take this cup!'
Holding the chipped mug the black King

Had drunk from out of the window
For the rain to spit in.

IX

What is Essential is Hostile to Life

Sometimes when she is playing one of her destructions,
    I hide.
I find wherever I imagine she does not know, and hide
With some books and some wine, and a few scratched
    old records . . .

But she always finds me, and is not amused,
And I see the vanity of my retreat, how pathetic a retreat
    is —
The wine, the books, the records — when it has been
    stormed.

'I am Siberia,' she said once, 'my cold gets everywhere!'
'You are too French for me,' I said. 'But we are . . . '
She smiled, 'But why should it be me who says what we
    are?'

'O my love,' she will croon, breaking the records one
    by one,
'O my muskrat,' she will murmur, pouring the wine
    away,
'O my own true husband,' she will say, setting all the
    books on fire.

X

'Where shall I hide from Lydia?' I cry,
'Not even Leviathan has a belly

Large and sea-sunken enough . . .
On the tallest tower of Babylon

She would find me out, my
King Kong with one piercing green eye . . .

Find me out and know me, and not in the Biblical
Sense either, but worse, far worse.'

I fall to my knees and say,
'I will be good to you!'

She laughs, 'You were never good in your life
Which has been blissfully devoted

To not being good or true to your friends.
It is this quality we love in you.'

One of her deadliest speeches . . .
How 'blissfully' spits from her!

So I shall not even hide in virtue.
So I shall not even cover my nakedness

In the twigs of charity that cover other men.
Was anyone more miserable?

'Yes,' Lydia says, 'many.
Many,' she repeats; I shrink. 'Many, many . . . '

I'm an ant now on one of her gloves. With one
Imperial gesture, she drops

But does not kill me. Even on the floor
I am conspicuous as crystal.

XI

'Look, Lydia,' I said, 'I am like one of those fishes
You find in the deepest Pacific –
The ones with little furry feelers and mouths

The size of footballs? Yes! Well (don't interrupt!)
They live in the dark and if you bring them up . . .'
'They burst,' she interrupts, 'they burst,'

Lying back on the bed and closing her eyes.
'Do you know how many times you've said this before?
Threatened to burst and burst

Until I face what a monster I am?
You've been threatening for years
But all you do is get fatter and more cruel.'

I start to cry, although I know she loves this part,
The way my tears swell in what she has called
(She can't deny it!) my 'brutal and beautiful' eyes.

'I DO deny it,' she is saying, 'I do deny
I called your eyes beautiful. Brutal, yes,
The eyes of all sentimentalists are brutal.'

'Don't you understand, Lydia, I really am'
(My voice is soft) 'one of those Pacific fishes.'
'You skulk at the bottom of the night, you mean –

So deep down no one can reach you.'
'Balls,' I say, stroking her left thigh,
'YOU get to me! You really do!'

'Say that again,' she says, 'it always amuses me
When you do the sincerity bit. Wide eyes, central vein
   staring . . . '

XII

Fernando as Joseph

'Having always been beautiful, brilliant, and witty
You can imagine, Lydia, how I had the spoiled thing

Of always imagining
Everyone in the end would HAVE to love me.

Yes, they would have to.
How could you resist Betelgeuse?

One day they would have to look up and see it shining
And say, "Well, that's it." Awe and reverence . . .

They would be happy, too,
When they found out how true

It was that I was superior in all things.
I'm running on. Amazing how exciting it can be

To revive an ancient vanity . . .
Well, Lydia, you know the story.

I got dumped in a pit.
Thrown right down, down, to the bottom of it

And left to slaver there and shake with fear.
How long? Years. And if I press my forehead,

Thus! It is because I still
Need to remember I am not dead

So awful was that time.
Are you listening?

There is an end to the story
Not miserable entirely.

I shall put on a tie to tell it,
One of those flamboyant French ties

Victor Hugo sent me
With dragons and birds.

I will need music too . . . '

'If you're going to tell me
What happens next, Fernando, I know

Already. Besides, it's late.
Besides, there is no pharaoh here,

No Jacob sobbing into his beard
To receive your blessing, no panoply

Spread out for either you or me . . .
It is the no-story

Robs you of words, honey.
Sit down,' she is saying, 'sit down near me.

Have a beer. Or some of the wine in the fridge.
Or anything at all.

Really it does not matter.
Dignity and happiness aren't everything.

Suffering without end or purpose,
Well, that,' she is saying, 'well, that . . . '

'Out with it, Lydia!'
She is laughing. 'No,

That would only be another, darker pit.
You might never crawl out of it.'

XIII

'What roles remain? Answer me!
I feel old. I feel dreary.

I've done it all, after all . . .
Slept with Caligula (twice!)

Traded epigrams with Erasmus.
I have worn my socks clean

I have worn them dirty.
I have passed the age of thirty.

Thinking of the Buddha
I have picked my nose!'

'Look in my mirror,' Lydia says (in prose),
'See Nobody there;

Laugh and despair,
Despair and laugh.'

'Supposing I don't laugh,' I said.
'I can't always promise to find my joie-de-vivre . . . '

'You'll have to
Or I'll laugh for you.'

XIV

Lydia, I laughed out loud in the rickety old bus,
Reading in my Nietzsche
'What moralists never dare understand
Is that the wicked are happy'
I laughed and was so happy
There is hope after all for both of us

I blessed each passing crow and tree
I blessed each child with rickets
Each screech of the bus tyres
I had an orgy of internal blessing

God I was so happy
Seeing everything I knew about us
Didn't matter at all
It could be a source of joy, the old Kraut was saying
All this wisdom of treachery, a source of JOY, capital J
Joy in lederhosen,
Eagle-and-sausage joy, joy all the year round
In the harsh white light,
In the green light, in every light . . .

And I fell to my knees in the bus
And blessed you too (this had to come)
For helping me to torture myself so thoroughly

(Only you, darling, could have done it!)
Screwing me to such a delicate wild pitch
That Nietzsche sings in my heart and soul
Hurting me to such an ecstasy of self-hatred
That here I am, a changed man,
Blessing all the old trousers
And shopping bags in the bus
Crying out 'Be wicked! Be happy!' under my breath

XV

'The dream I had last night! It moved me so!
You and I were both silent,

Walking silently through snow
Snow was falling, silent, slow . . . '

'The rhymes,' Lydia says, 'they're sending me to sleep!
Is that what they are meant to do?'

'My dream, my visionary dream . . .
Don't you want to know

What you were doing, how the sky
Went purple and gold around us, how, at one moment,
  . a deer – '

'A deer? . . . Don't tell me, "with huge and shining eyes"?'
'Yes,' I said. 'Yes,' she said, 'and the deer TALKED,
   didn't it?'

I said nothing. What could I say?
'Really, a deer with "huge shining eyes"

Talking in the snow at us . . .
Was there a crucifix between its antlers

Or did it just sermonise like Balaam's ass?
Ha ha,' she goes mirthlessly, 'ha ha.

I don't dig revelations,
They tend to veer toward the banal I find.'

'Yes,' I said, 'it talked beautifully.
It talked Latin.'

'Naturally,' Lydia said.
'The Agnus Dei,' I said. 'Naturally,

What else would a deer be saying?'
'And you, Lydia, were kneeling in the snow by it,
   praying

And weeping.'
'In your dreams, Fernando

I am always praying and weeping.'

XVI

Is this how Lydia saves me, mocking me always
Away from myself, so when I am, for instance,

'Smelling my way to Dover' she is laughing,
'You look like a monkey'?

And when I am Nebuchadnezzar
(Which I am often), the mad king grovelling

Among the grasshoppers, all she will do
Is peel a grape, or dance to some vacant tune

On her wind-up gramophone? Oh Lydia
Charmless One, Goddess Beady Eye

There is nothing I am or long to be
You cannot mock and dissolve. 'Exactly.

See things as they are
And turn to stone.'

'Stone, Lydia, stone?'
(I beard her on everything! I am my own man!)

'Is it only as stone
I shall not harm anyone?'

I say it so sweetly, in such a small voice,
It would make even Nero cry.

'Yes,' says Lydia. Then silence.
'Yes,' again. 'As stone.'

She is speaking like a sibyl this afternoon
In sweaty, loaded fragments.

'Only as stone.' It tolls like a bell . . .
'But Lydia,' I cry,

'I must live and love,
I must love and live . . . '

'Why?' says Lydia. 'What good have you alive
Done anyone? Who has your love

Not harmed?' I name a childhood cat, two flies
I saved last summer, one flower . . .

It is not enough. Even I see that.
The names dry in my throat.

'Oh Lydia, Goddess, let me live!'
'Why not? Dogs and rats have life . . . '

And: 'Turning to stone
Isn't hard –

You have to see how helpless you are.
How helpless, and alone!

Then it comes easy,
easy as breath . . . '

XVII

'At least I am honest,' I say. 'You'll give me that.'
'Why should I give you anything?

Could Nebuchadnezzar not eat grass?
Could Jane Russell hide her breasts and ass?

You are what you are.
You are what you are condemned to be.'

'Do you never think, Lydia, I do it well?
That I bring to the dance of my despair

A je-ne-sais-quoi both moving and rare?'
'Wash your mouth out,' she says. 'I mean

Out, out, wash it away . . .
Kill your applauding fool, you fool,

Pray every night
As you fall asleep in his arms

You'll wake to find him dead
At the bottom of the bed.'

'You put it well. I must take it down.'
'Do what the hell you like,

But know this for certain, my friend,
An end will come only when you make an end.'

'Until then . . . what?' I say, farouche, yes, but
    half-afraid.
'Until then – this . . .

Is *this* what you want,
Wriggling and sizzling

In the fat of your despair?'
'*Quelle phrase*, Lydia,

"Wriggling and sizzling" – well done!
I am taking it, I promise you,

I am take-take-taking it down.'

XVIII

Lydia as the Witch of Endor

One particularly bloody dusk we went to the cupboard
And dragged out all my mother's and grandmother's

Old dresses – the ones with ragged ermine capes –
A hat with six moth-eaten cherries on it, a parasol

Whose tip was red coral, from the tip of India.
'Well,' Lydia said, 'shall I begin?

Today I am the Witch of Endor and you are Saul
Though god knows why we have to go through this farce

Since we both know the story.' 'O dear Lydia,' I say,
'How literal you are. With an eternity to kill

How can a little play-acting harm?
Even this story has its charm,

The mad witch speaking what the old king knows
Dissolving his false poetry with her prose . . . '

'Do you really want', she asks
'The full recital, how your loves and joys will end

Tomorrow in a darkened wind,
How all things for which you've worked and sinned . . . ?'

'Yes,' I said. 'I do.
It gives me a kick to hear it from you.

You do the grisly thing so well
I love the way your voice curls when you say "end",

How you shimmy your earrings when you bend
And touch the floor and scream "Death Death Death" –

How do you ever find the breath?
Did Saul invent Her as I do you

To keep him company as his life goes bad?'
'Invent me!' She is furious. 'Invent me!'

Lydia was larger than me already
And soon became larger even than the room.

Her eyes were furnaces!
'No man', she roared, 'entirely invents his doom!'

Then (shrinking back to size)
'You don't need me

To tell you what you know already –
It's curtains, baby.'

'Curtains?' I repeated, 'Curtains?'
Thinking of my grandmother's white lace curtains
   (such is memory)

Thinking (such is the cultured mind)
Of the curtains Polonius was killed behind . . .

'Curtains,' Lydia said, drawing them, leaving the lights off.
I write affectedly, but with shaking hand

(In this, at least, I may still have a choice),
'Someone in the street is screaming with my voice . . . '

XIX

'Try a neutral subject,' Lydia said, 'I'm tired . . . '
Such a sweet confession.

How almost-beautiful she looked, those scanning
Palomar eyes closed for once

(Close your eyes, Lydia, let language and its stars go
    out),
Her hands folded on her stomach, like hands

On a tomb by Pisano.
'My love,' I said, 'neutrality is hard to learn

After years of – '
'Crap,' she said. 'And why do you always talk

Like a theologian from Kansas?' 'Kansas?' I cried,
'There are no theologians in Kansas,'

And 'What the hell do you know about theology?'
We bitched for a full hour on THAT one . . .

All this started as my attempt –
Considering the purity of this winter sunlight

Considering the beneficent gaiety of the squirrels
Considering the white and tender face of the lawn –

To write one poem in which
Lydia is not 'Lydia Rampant', acute and brutal.

'Ha!' says Lydia suddenly revived, searching
For the words that kill –

'You're boring them.'

XX

She nibbles my ear. 'What have you written?'
I say, 'Nothing,' and it is true,
I have written nothing all morning.

'Ah,' she whispers, 'to have written Nothing –
That would be something!'
I groan. 'Yes,' she says, 'to have found

The words for this final morning
These rocks in their peeled heaven
This one cornflower pure as snow . . .

And then to have written it all
To reveal also
The large abyss of air

Behind and around everything . . .
That would be something.'
Adding: 'You will have to do better

Than "large abyss of air", MUCH better.'
I sit straight-backed: 'Today
No abysses concern me.

Today I am wordlessness and levity.'
She laughs: 'You say you are happy so grimly!'
And laughs and laughs.
So I stand up and write:

'There will be nothing written this morning
But what the morning writes
On everything that lives and moves,
The name of a Nothingness no one can write!'

'Ha,' she says. '*Very* eloquent.'

XXI

Lament

'By the waters of Babylon I sat down and . . . '
'Shat,' said Lydia loudly.

'Lydia, really! You are not usually . . . '
'You shat and that was that.'

'I wept,' I said, starting to.
'You know I did.'

Here Lydia yawns. 'You shat.
You ate, drank, fucked, and shat.'

Why should I accept that?
I do have a choice!

I say, 'By the waters of Babylon, Lydia,
I sat . . . '

(Waiting for it . . .)
'I was dignified and stricken

And I wept, as I weep now.' Lydia smiles, says nothing.
'As I weep now,' I repeat, by force of repetition

Forcing a few tears. 'As I weep now.'
Lydia keeps smiling, stares out of the window.

A week later, it seems, she starts and says
'Why didn't you just *leave* Babylon?

Just get on a bus and leave?' I am shocked.
Doesn't Lydia know there are no buses out of Babylon?

Just how unhistorical *is* she?
'Why didn't you leave?

You wept, you watched yourself weeping,
In the still, glittering water . . .

That kept you captive.
The old story! You stored your tears like pearls,

Such pearls! To cast before – such swine! – in chains
Of Tragic, Tortured Song.'

She spat neatly into the tears at my feet.
'Well, *that's* over. Now I, Lydia, have come

With my stone hands
To wipe your eyes white –

By the waters of Babylon you shall sit down,
See your reflection, shit, and run.'

I looked up to savage her. She was gone.
Slowly, I looked down.

XXII

'I am Callas! Today I am finally Callas!
My voice is flame and tears! I shout "Assassino!"

From the top of the stairs
And all the rabbits in the wallpaper die!

I stand above the toilet
I raise my jewelled dagger, shout "T'odio, t'odio"

And the body of Lydia, vast as the Southern Hemisphere,
Falls flaming into the abyss, leaking sawdust and marbles . . .

Who could have imagined

One of my mother's taffetas, and some rouge,
Could have done so much for me?

Or that on one black coffee
My tenor could have found such high 'C's, so high, so wild

They fall from the heights like napalm . . . '
'Sit down,' says Lydia. 'You should see yourself . . .

Is this what a little taffeta does for you?
Sit down, Fernando,

You're sweating and not making a sound.'
And it was true.

XXIII

'It was in another country, and besides
The pillar has fallen . . . '

'What are you on about?'
'Today,' I said, 'I am enigmatic, composed

In orders of mourning beyond your reach.
It was in another country . . . '

'Oh I know,' she smiles.
'You're remembering when

You were Simeon Stylites. (That jerk!)
In the desert on one leg for years!

How funny you were
Waiting for the dead of night

To change positions, barking the vultures away
When they swooped too close – and not in Latin, either.

How piqued, too,
When no one came

To admire your game!
From where I was sitting I could see distinctly

Your lips blacken from self-pity!'
'From where you were SITTING!' I exploded.

'Lydia, you were *there*
Jostling me off the pillar,

Wheeling about me,
Whirring obscenities in my ear . . .

Remember the time when
You got yourself up as Helen

And strutted round my pillar naked?
Call that sitting? And when

You were the Patriarch and sang songs to my sanctity
And nearly made me "come down and be free"?'

'Just be grateful, you idiot,
Someone took you half-seriously.'

'Someone!' I cried. 'The whole civilised world . . . '
'Crap. You were USED. You were a SHOW.

People came to look at you when they had nowhere else
    to go.
You were a film and you got BORING, you know,

Saying nothing up there and standing on one leg.
Besides, playing the saintly flamingo alone

Would have sent you cuckoo.
I entertained you; for many a day and night

I was the only half-true friend you had!'
'With such friends as you . . . '

'Without me', she said, 'you'd be mad.
You'd be BORING and mad.

Get down on your one remaining knee
Call out my name and bless me.'

I knelt, I whispered weakly, 'Lydia! Lydia!'
'Louder!' she cried. 'Louder . . .

Look up now, Fernando,
Here's the Pope to see you!'

XXIV

'Crisp, void and flat are all the oblivions, Lydia,
That gape for our ideals and loves.

Romeos, read that and sob!

Roll wounded on that bed of salt
Unmasked pomposopher, and howl.'

'Goodness,' says Lydia. 'What's bitten you?'
'The Real,' I answer proudly, and expose my roses –

The four little marks the Real made last night
One on each nipple, and two between my legs.

'The Real has wounded and healed me.
The Real has robbed me of all words, Lady,

And spoken these through me . . . '
'You're crazy

And in, I'm afraid, the dullest way – '
'Not so as I can see . . .

If I go on this way
I might well out-Nietzsche Nietzsche.

Now the Real has bitten me and I have lived
Is there anything on earth I cannot be?

There is nothing, I can see . . . '
Snuggling down into my sofa . . .

'Exactly,' says Lydia.

XXV

'You're making pasta', I said, 'out of my deepest
    beliefs!'
What balls to have said it at last!

Each shoulder grew by three inches . . .
I found I almost had a moustache

(I've always wanted a moustache).

'That's what "deepest beliefs" are for,' she said.
Can you believe it? My voice went red

And ran for cover under the bed . . .
My almost-moustache? It went white . . .

'I'm a wreck,' I said. She said, 'It's night,
No one can see you. We're quite alone . . .

If it really is white – '
She said, 'And I can't see in the night –

You'll bless me. Old age can't be far,
Not in *time* necessarily' (warming to her theme)

'But in a certain *weight* of pain and rage.
Old age,' she smiled, 'and the blessed end of old age.'

XXVI

A Little Night Music

I would like to write; I have risked my sanity
Writing these poems. There, I've written it . . .

'If only you had,' she drawls. 'Vanity, vanity
Even here. Besides who cares about your sanity

So long as the poems ring true.'
'I care!' I shout. 'I care! I care terrifically!'

'Ah,' she says, 'you care about something after all.
It would be something to do with you . . .

What good did your damn sanity ever do?
The holiest fools seem mad, Fernando,

They tilt at windmills and speak so wisely
The rest of the world must think they're crazy . . . '

Lydia is smiling. She does not mean what she says,
And says so. 'The holy ones, of course,

Are the most boring. On and on about Virtue,
The Kingdom of the Just,

How Lazarus can bounce up from the dust –
Thank god we know better, don't we?

I mean,' she says, 'we are modern,' peeling a grape.

I balk at that, my arms start to shiver and wave,
I find myself growing a goatee like Quixote . . .

'That won't work, I'm afraid.
All you will be left tomorrow, you'll see,

Is an even balder sanity.
Here, take the grape, beloved, do!

The little foxes have stripped the vines bare
But I'm still good for a muscat or two.'

XXVII

'It's *such* a relief not to be proud any more
Or if a little proud then not on the scale, say,

Of Hannibal trying to eat through the Alps with vinegar
Or Xerxes setting an army of mattocks on Mount Athos

Or Belisarius still raving and arrogant at Beggar's Bush
Or Bajazet . . . ' 'MUST I listen to this bilge all day?'

(Lydia doesn't read much, you see.)
'I just wanted you to be grateful', I say,

'That you don't have a really full-fledged
Monster on your hands – just a human, mortal, guilty

But not wholly monstrous.' 'So that's it,' she said,
'*That* is the end of classical learning; there's always

An example handy to get you off the hook . . .
Why didn't you mention Nero or Caligula?

To be monstrous on THAT scale, you need wit
And have to *work* at it –

And when have you, Fernando, worked at anything?
To be a monster', she said, 'is hard as being a saint.'

'You picked that up', I said,
'From some Frenchie. Sounds smart

But it isn't really.'
'I love it when you argue,' Lydia says,

'Your lips turn down; your eyes narrow like a pig's.'
'Turdus sibi malum cacat . . . ' I say.

Lydia claps. 'It's Latin now . . . what's it mean?'
'Evil lays its own turd. You are my turd,

My huge speaking turd, and you stink at me.'
'What a big boy you are using such bad words!

So true and so dirty!
How proud you must be.'

XXVIII

I write: 'The belief that anything fulfils
Is what kills.'

Yes. I savour the rhyme.
I take out an imaginary cigar and remember the line

'Je fume mon cigare devant les fortifications.'
I savour the line, the rhyme. I savour my cigar.

And Lydia naturally is sitting opposite me, waiting.
'What are you waiting for?' I ask.

I open some books of French poetry:
I offer her an imaginary cigar

(Not a gesture calculated to charm her).
I repeat: 'The belief that anything fulfils

Is what kills.' 'Kills what?' she asks.
'Life, Lydia, and the truth of life.'

'Which is what?' Lydia is demure today, it seems.
Almost humble. 'Death,' I say.

Si le grain ne meurt . . .

Lydia is making strange sounds . . .
'I am dying inwardly,' she says, in a strangled voice.

I'm furious. 'How dare you mock me!
How dare you despise my spiritual intensity?'

The stigmata begin to appear on my left hand . . .
'Despise it?' Lydia says. 'My dear,

My feelings are duller, I fear.'
I produce the stigmata in silence. They are my trump
   cards.

Damn the rhyme, the cigar. No one could be so hard
As to deny the force of such a love.

The birds are singing louder now.
One tree, I see, begins to blossom in their song.

Lydia is saying nothing. She takes my imaginary cigar.
She puts her feet up on my desk, staring at me.

How little it takes
To make me a wreck.

Look how she makes the smoke-rings
Fall like nooses round my neck.

XXIX

'To have a mind like a mirror, Lydia,
Going after nothing

Welcoming nothing
Responding but not storing . . .

Seeing the squirrel as a squirrel
And not a flashing actor of my will

Hearing nothing but wind in the wind
Finding no traces of my face

In the wind-pillared, wind-scripted snow.
I must vanish, Lydia,

Or be hunted to my hole
And killed; must throw myself away, I know

Or be gathered to destructions
My mind will break at – '

'Yes,' says Lydia,
'And this is one of them . . . ' handing me her mirror.

'Say it all over,
I love it when you play the sage.

There are so few true pleasures –
Why miss the way your face

Hardens to a mask and lies, and lies,
When you talk wise?'

XXX

'Today,' I say, 'when the snows have melted,
When the memory of last night's moon

So high in its clear and brilliant sky
Still shines in us,

When the garden is shining,
When all the squirrels have left their solitudes

To run unrestrained
Along the bare and lustrous branches of the oak tree,

Today, our music, Lydia, should be
Perfect, a harmony

Of will and desire, hunger and fulfilment,
The full music, Lydia, the philosophers speak of

That is not known or heard until the heart is clear,
That cannot be sounded

Until all the senses are dancing,
Until the ideal conjunction of Virgo and Mercury . . . '

I wave my hands. I summon Lydia to begin.
She says: 'That you spoke at all

Ruins everything.'

XXXI

Once More unto the Breach

What a luxury to pray for one's enemy!
How warm my epiglottis feels as the prayers

Trickle down my throat like old French brandy!
'May She who mocks and calumniates me', I pray,

'Also attain Nirvana with me.
May She who has made of my life a misery

Also be healed in the Void.'
Lydia shakes me sharply.

'No Void for me, honey.
As for Nirvana,

You can stuff it . . . And as for
Going with you or anyone,

If I go I want to be alone.'
'May She who denies and destroys me – '

'Are you crazy?
Or just trying to anger me?'

'As if I, Lydia,
Would talk to the Buddha

Just to anger you! What vanity!'
Something I said makes Lydia smile . . .

'Talk to WHO did you say?'
'Lydia, please, no arguments today . . . '

'Talk to WHO?' She is adamant. She is blazing.
58

XXXII

Spiders love Mozart, someone told me. ·
So I try Mozart out on Lydia.

'*Dalla sua pace*' very loud . . .
Is Mozart not a proof of the existence of God?

Is Mozart not a Sign that something in Man
Is higher than the frog?

And that I listen to Mozart (Lydia, look at me!)
With an expression of such mature serenity

Does that not also –
'Let the man sing, Fernando,

But don't talk.
Let the man sing

But don't say
It has anything to do with anything.

Spiders love Mozart, someone told you.
Now you know it's true.'

'Really,' I began, 'that's going too far!'
But the sweet song was over.

XXXIII

Il Mio Tesoro

'Don't leave me . . . .' 'Look,' she says,
'If I stay I do not stay *with* you

If I leave, I do not leave *you*.
Is that clear?' She lights a cigarette.

She is beautiful in the half–light.
'What does it matter', she says,

'If I am beautiful or not?
It is not my beauty that matters.

Sometimes you see me as Cleopatra.
Sometimes it is only the Gorgon you see.

All that is boring to me . . .'
'So then you do love me,' I whisper,

'Somewhere at the heart of your violence
There is a small ruby of fidelity

We have made together,'
' "Ruby of fidelity", what kind of

Horseshit is that?
I am neither faithful nor unfaithful.

Why must you find words for me?
Are you afraid, Fernando,

To let me be?'
She laughs: 'To let me be . . . Ha! With each category

You make another pyre
To try and burn me on . . .

But I am not Dido, mourning, magnificent,
Disposable for your master-plan.

You see, I will not burn.'
'Lydia,' I say, 'listen to me.

How can you say I only want
To burn you alive?'

I put on my charming voice,
The voice I learnt at school, the voice with which

I might seduce the Furies . . .
' "Seduce the Furies!" ' She laughs,

'You can't seduce them.
That is their gift, the misery

They bring, which you cannot flee.'
'You are their gift, too, I suppose?'

'Yes,' she says, 'in a way.'
Then: 'Leave out the Dido bit,

It is too theatrical, too grand.
We are much more intimate . . . '

Walking slowly towards me
Putting out her cigarette in my inkstand.

XXXIV

If God exists and is a child, as sometimes I think,
A wanton, radiant child who makes and re-makes rules,

Worlds, universes, to his whim, a child who moves Time
Playing draughts with it, our lives, our thoughts, our
    identities . . .

If God is this child, I say, Lydia is his playmate.
'So that is what you say,' she says. 'Ha! So I get to play

With God in this poem. That's something for a
    Brooklyn girl.'
'But you're not from Brooklyn,' I say. 'Of course not,'
    she says,

'Why do you always take me literally?'
This is where I get angry —

What else can a man do? I have given the bitch divine
    status
And all she can do is make jokes about Brooklyn

Which she hasn't even been to. 'So what if I take you
    literally?
So what?' I get butch. I stand up . . .

'Look,' she says, 'leave God out of it. Look back at
    those first five lines.
Isn't there something too plump and egregious about
    them?'

'What does egregious mean?' 'I don't know,' she says,
'And frankly, by this time (for it was night

And there wasn't a tender star in sight)
'I don't give a damn. Leave God out of it anyway,'

She says, humming something to herself. 'Why in hell,
Lydia, are you humming at a time like this?

Aren't souls at stake? Aren't the most important
    questions
Poised like kingfishers somewhere in this room

Ready to dive and take the tops of our heads off?
If God is a child and you are his playmate . . . '

'Cut this crap,' she says. 'I never wanted to be
    immortal.'
'What do you want?' I cried. 'What is it you want?'

'I could say Truth,' she says, 'but you would spell it
    wrong.
I could say, "What does any Brooklyn girl want?"

But you'd think I was making some kind of joke.
I could of course say nothing, but you, you fool,

Would think that was kind of, somehow, important.'

XXXV

'Fantasy is my Persepolis and I shall
Burn it down.' 'Your what?' asked Lydia. 'What's
   Persepolis?'

Sometimes I despair of her, she is so ignorant.
'Well, dear Lydia, there was this king called
   Alexander . . . '

'Oh him, you talk about him in your sleep
As if he were a friend . . . ' 'He is! That's it exactly!'

'Why do you have incendiarists for friends?'
It is her turn to smile sweetly

(Picking her teeth). 'And this Persepolis . . . '
'It was a city,' I intoned,

'Fair and majestic, with hanging gardens,
Seraglios, troupes of saltimbanques.'

'And he burnt down the lot?' she asked. 'The whole
   thing?'
'Yes. Nothing remained. "Above the sad waste

Eagles were seen to dip and hover, their golden heads
Dark with mourning." ' Lydia starts laughing . . .

'Those weren't eagles, they were vultures,
You don't have to know anything to know that.

Why did he burn it down?' 'It was his enemy's city,
He was drunk.' 'And you, sweetheart' (she is loving
    tonight)

'Are you drunk?'
'You know very well I'm dead sober.'

'Then you can't do it.' 'What?' 'Burn Persepolis down.'
'Try me,' I say, thickening my voice, getting my lighter
    ready . . .

'It's either', she said, huskily,
'The saltimbanques

Or the vultures – take your pick . . . '
'You always think in opposites,' I say, 'it makes me sick!'

'Take your pick,' she repeats, 'Magic or Death –
Let the hanging gardens hang. You'll go crazy,

But they'll be a good setting, Fernando,
All those aromatic roses and gazebos.'

(She is smiling) 'Besides, with Persepolis gone
Where would I get my tiger-striped silks?'

'Damn your silks! Walk naked.' 'Naked?' she laughed,
'Did I hear you ask me to walk naked?

The sight of me naked, sweetheart – bear this in mind –
Would burn you deaf, dumb, and blind.'

XXXVI

'Don't think I don't appreciate what you're doing for me,
Lydia . . . it's amazing really,

Your anger, your concern . . . '
I take out a cigar. I watch it burn.

'It's just that I keep thinking of Socrates, Lydia,'
(How pleasant to think of Socrates

On days as spring-like as these!)
'Of how he lived for wisdom . . . '

Here I leaned forward –
'Yet who did he change?

Jesus too,' I added. 'So much passion wasted. Such a
    shame.'
The cigar is perfect. I smoke it slowly . . .

'And so you really think,' Lydia says,
'I grieve for your soul . . .

There are weeks, no, *years*
I can't remember your name.'

XXXVII

No Diamonds, No Hat, No Honey

'This is it; this is what I have discovered.'
(Lydia already has one of her ears covered.)

'You must love the bitch Reality
In all her stinking rags and face of stone!

You must face her, by God, face her naked and alone!'
'What have you been drinking?' Lydia asks, and then –

'Let me finish this, I bet I can . . .
"Face the bitch and hold her and still say 'Yes',"

Is that what you were going to say? Confess!'
It was. I was ashamed. 'Oh God,' Lydia says. 'And
    then?

What the hell happens then?' I improvise, I say,
'It's simple, Lydia, the hag changes, she has to,

It's not magical, it's law –
The hag becomes the queen with the diamond hat.'

Mentally, of course, I'm thinking, 'Beat that,
You bitch,' but go on, quite in the flow,

'Yes, the stone becomes a stone, the snow the snow,
Everything is at once diamond and the same,

Kind of.' It *did* sound lame –
Why did I bother?

'You face the hag or you don't.
You hold her to you or you don't.

No diamonds, no hat, no honey. You do it
Or you don't. Pour me a drink.'

'A question of dignity then,' I say. 'Kind of . . . '
'Nothing kind about that,' Lydia says,

'Pour me a drink, I said . . .
This is not the kind of talk we have on a clear head.'

XXXVIII

Lydia walks towards me . . .
Thank God there's a holy tamarisk tree

I can sit down under. So I do.
Lydia breathes into my ear.

'And what do you have to say now?'
But this time – ha! – I'll not fall prey to her.

I shall sit and smile silently like the Buddha
Hold out my silence to her as a big fat sunflower.

Hope it chokes her!
Let the worlds revolve around *my* navel for a bit

And the moon hop in the grass around me like a rabbit.
I need a bit of confidence. I need it bad.

If I don't get it I might well go . . .
No more of that. Back to the silence thing,

To the sunflower and the tamarisk tree.
Lydia is sitting close now. She has undone my shirt.

She is whispering, 'Won't you miss me?
Who will you talk to when you're holy?'

My chest is jittery. She smells of myrrh . . .
Oh Lord, I pray, let it not be with her

I have to share what garden may remain.
'But it is,' she answers,

'However you mix the myths,' she says,
'I'll always be in them.'

XXXIX

Coda

'All afternoon my tears fell for Scott of the Antarctic.
All men have their secrets; this is one of mine.

For Scott the man, and those last words of his
Written in the final wind

"I do not regret this last journey; we took risks, we
    knew
We took them . . . " ' I can't go on. Already, Lydia is
    pacing

With that stare that foretells
A doom less kind than death. 'Go on,' she smiles, 'let
    the tears

Fall to the end . . . ' My eyes swim, I stagger, I say,
' "Things have come out against us; therefore, we have

No cause for complaint." ' Lydia laughs. I am angry.
'Who could say any more? This is nobility!

This is the courage that rails against nothing,
Accepting in the soul's Latin what has been given.'

Lydia is deathly tonight, the moonlight lies along
Her arms like ice . . . 'Oh,' she mocks,

'How men adore the classic types.' Then, 'I like the
    phrase
"In the soul's Latin".' Then, 'He had to say something,

Didn't he, out in the waste like that,
Stripped of everything but the hope

Of some poor idiot's tears . . . ' She is tired suddenly.
She sits down. 'When will men understand, Fernando,

Nothing they say does not cheapen them —
Including what I have just said?'

Her eyes were so sad I was frightened.

'Clear these poems of all their words,' I hear her say.
'Let the snow that is falling cover us and them,

Let the night that is falling cover the snow also.'
'What then?' She smiles. 'How should I know?

"I do not regret this last journey; we took risks . . . " '